Racing a Ghost Ship

The Incredible Journey of Great American II

Rich Wilson

Walker and Company
New York

To Mom,
whose lifelong adventures continue to inspire me

First published in the United States of America in 1996 by Walker Publishing Company, Inc.
Published simultaneously in Canada by Thomas Allen & Son Canada, Limited, Markham, Ontario

Library of Congress Cataloging-in-Publication Data
Wilson, Rich.
Racing a ghost ship: the incredible journey of *Great American II* / Rich Wilson.
p. cm.
Includes index.
Summary: Relates the journey of two skippers who set sail from San
Francisco, navigated around Cape Horn, and arrived in Boston in time
to beat the previous speed record.
ISBN 0-8027-8415-1 (hardcover). —ISBN 0-8027-8417-8 (reinforced)
1. Wilson, Rich—Journeys.   2. Voyages around the world. 3. Great
American II (Sailboat)   [1. Wilson, Rich. 2. Voyages around the
world. 3. Great American II (Sailboat)]   I. Guernsey, JoAnn Bren.
II. Title.
G440.W746W55 1996
910.4'1—dc20
96-1914
CIP
AC

Special thanks to JoAnn Bren Guernsey for her fine editing.

Photographs on endpapers, title page, copyright page, and
contents page by Bill Biewenga/Stock Newport

Book design by Janice Noto-Helmers

Printed in Hong Kong

10 9 8 7 6 5 4 3 2 1

Contents

A Persistent Dream

My first attempt in 1990 at sailing around Cape Horn ended in disaster. Four hundred miles short of the Horn, I capsized in a horrendous storm. I lost my boat and very nearly my life. After a dramatic midnight rescue, I could only watch helplessly as my beautiful trimaran, *Great American*, slipped away into the black night. Dry and safe, I waited weeks before I started to plan my next attempt.

Many people asked me *why?* Even my own mother (who's quite an adventurer herself) said, "Richie, is it really necessary?" My answer became easier the more often I was asked. "Yes. It's my dream. If you have a dream, you go after it."

Nothing was more natural for me than sailing as I grew up. This was partly because my family lived in the sailing community of Marblehead, Massachusetts, and also because my father developed a passion for the sport. (He wallpapered my room with nautical charts—how could I resist such an open invitation to far horizons?) But the sea also appealed to me because I was allergic to just about everything on land. In the clean air at sea, I could breathe. And I could compete.

I'd had severe asthma since I was about a year old, and the medications and inhalers available during my childhood weren't nearly as good as they are now. Even if asthma didn't make me stop wanting to keep up with the other kids, it did mean I had to work harder at most sports. With sailing I didn't have to worry so much about physical limitations.

[childhood pictures by John J. Wilson]

5

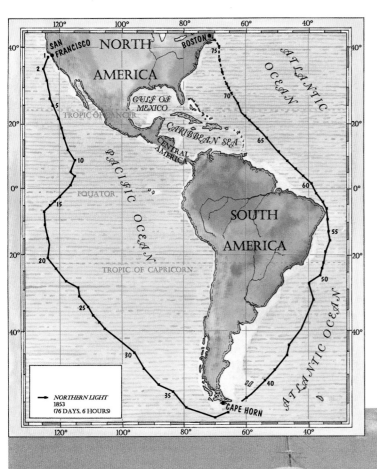

The challenge of sailing is twofold; you need skill and will. Acquiring the technical sailing ability is demanding enough. But the will? That is what's in your heart. When the vast sea gets its grip on you, it forces you to face its challenge.

Are you up to it?

My intended voyage was from San Francisco to Boston, around legendary Cape Horn—the grave-yard of countless ships and sailors. It would be more than 15,000 miles, nonstop and unassisted, with only one other crew member. And it would be a race

[Dennis O'Brien]

Northern Light
[painting by William Bradford, Hart Nautical Collection, MIT Museum]

against another ship—a phantom. I wanted to beat the speed record of seventy-six days set in 1853 by the great clipper ship *Northern Light*.

But nightmarish memories became a major part of the challenge for me. As I prepared for the January 1993 departure of *Great American II*, my mind replayed the images and sounds and fears from the capsizing of the first *Great American*, two years earlier.

Great American   [Billy Black]

Leap for the Ladder

Great American departs San Francisco on October 22, 1990, bound for Boston by way of Cape Horn.   [Phil Steggall]

Facing page: Cape Horn shrouded in fog.
[Gordon Gahan/National Geographic Society]

Thanksgiving Day, 1990. My coskipper, Steve Pettengill, and I had been approaching Cape Horn with forecasts of moderately rough gales. But as we closed to within 400 miles of the Horn, the wind shrieked and howled, building from 50 knots to 60, 70, and 80 knots, pushing the seas from 30 feet to 40, 50, and 60 feet high.

In these winds and mountainous waves, we covered 700 miles in 70 hours despite having no sails up and drag lines over the side to reduce our speed.

What a sport sailing is! No time-outs when the game plan breaks down; no substitutes when exhaustion sets in; no referee to keep things fair—just another thousand walls of water that want to do you in.

On one fateful wave the boat got turned sideways. She tilted to what seemed the point of no return, paused, and then, to our horror, kept going until, almost gently, she turned upside down. The cabin ceiling was now underfoot, and we found ourselves knee-deep in 41-degree water. Luckily we weren't hurt. After helping each other into our bulky neoprene survival suits to protect ourselves from the cold water, we activated our satellite distress signal and hoped that it would transmit through the fiberglass hull.

An hour later, without warning, a wave that must have been far higher than all the others wrenched the big trimaran out of the water, threw her upright, and slammed her violently down again.

I was launched upward and my head hit the floor. When I came to, I was underwater not knowing which way was up. Flailing around in every direction at once, I finally burst through the surface and heard Steve yelling for me. Now we were neck-deep in water, but, amazingly, we were again unhurt.

Everything, including all our radio and computer equipment, was underwater.

"Let's get out of here," Steve shouted. On deck, the huge mast had been torn into three separate pieces and lay hanging over the stern into the water. We took refuge in the forward sail locker, and I steadied myself by making plans for the next day: We'd get rid of the mast and start pumping out the 20,000 pounds of water. We weren't done yet.

In the middle of the night, even through the crashing storm, I gradually became aware of a different sound—a low, repeated moaning—a ship's horn! I opened the hatch and saw the lights of a wildly rolling ship. It was *New Zealand Pacific*, the world's largest refrigerated container ship (815 feet long—think of a skyscraper laid down on its side). Notified of our distress call, the ship had rushed 100 miles to find us. The seas continued to rage, however, and boarding a ship in such conditions could have been more deadly than staying where we were. What were they going to do?

Facing page: **An angry, churning sea.**
[Gordon Gahan/National Geographic Society]

[Dennis O'Brien]

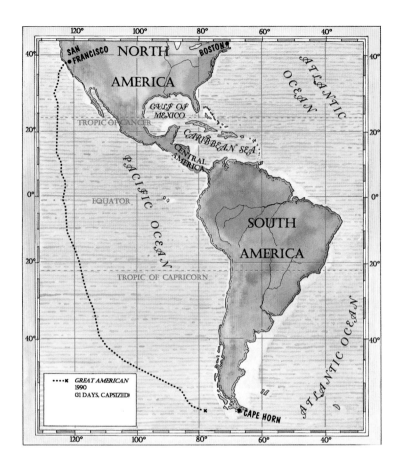

When the ship came within 300 yards of us, I could see a lit door open in the ship's side, 20 feet above the water. The captain maneuvered his ship brilliantly, and it soon became clear that he was bringing his 62,000-ton ship alongside to pick us up!

When it was about 30 yards away, two ropes snaked through the darkness, and we heard a shout to tie the lines around ourselves.

Time to go. We climbed out of the hatch, crawled across the deck, tied the lines, and watched the massive black wall of steel, now only 15 yards away. A rope ladder hung from the door, and cargo netting from the deck above. Now 10 yards, 5 yards, then the ship touched *Great American*'s pontoon, positioned perfectly.

Lifted by the next huge wave, we rode the trimaran up the side of the ship like an elevator. I chased away dark thoughts of missing my jump and falling into the water, or of being crushed between the two vessels. I told myself, *We've only got one shot at this*. "Now!" I yelled to Steve. I leaped for the

ladder and Steve for the netting. We both got firm grips and climbed for our lives. Friendly hands pulled us in the door. Before it was closed, we took one last look at our third shipmate, *Great American*. For thirty days we had guided her and she had defended us. She'd done two somersaults and hadn't broken up on us. She was down by the stern but her bow was high and proud. We said an emotional thank you . . . and good-bye.

Facing page: *New Zealand Pacific*—each of the small, rectangular boxes on the ship's deck is the size of a tractor-trailer truck.　　[P & O Containers]

Sharing the Adventure

One of my favorite things to do—discussing the voyage with students who followed *Great American II.*   [Lyon Osborn]

The voyage of *Great American* had been followed by students in 1,000 classrooms nationwide through a newsletter. When we returned, after the capsize and rescue, I visited many of these classes. Even though we had not achieved our goal, it was obvious to me that the students' interest had been hooked on our voyage. And their interest and enthusiasm, more than anything else, persuaded me to try again.

If the voyage had just been to try to set a record, I wouldn't have tried it. It had to be of benefit to others. I wanted to inspire people, especially children, to reach for their own dreams. I was convinced that people of all ages, even those who had never seen the ocean, would enjoy a gripping adventure, especially if they could watch it unfold, day by day, with real people in real time. Nobody would know the outcome of this race and journey until it ended.

Students at St. Joseph's Junior High School in Manchester, New Hampshire, display the topographically accurate relief map of North and South America that they built.

[St. Joseph's Junior High School]

This time, with the voyage of *Great American II*, we wanted to reach more people. We persuaded twelve major newspapers to distribute a curriculum based on our voyage to teachers in 10,000 classrooms (250,000 students nationwide) who "joined" us on board. Schoolchildren could follow our progress aboard *GA II* on maps, alongside a path representing the historic voyage of *Northern Light*. I would write a weekly column from *GA II* for these newspapers that would go to the classrooms and also be read by their 13 million readers.

Three times each week I would write a log for, and answer questions from, students on the Prodigy computer network. We'd also report in daily on 1-900-820-BOAT, a phone line available nationwide. Money received from the 900 calls would be used to support the satellite communications costs. We genuinely wanted to let people in on our voyage. That commitment was certain to keep us very busy.

As the day of departure approached, I realized just how many people were counting on me. Would those extra eyes and ears help to strengthen my resolve, or make my task all the more difficult?

Facing page: *Great American II* **from the masthead.**
[Bill Biewenga/Stock Newport]

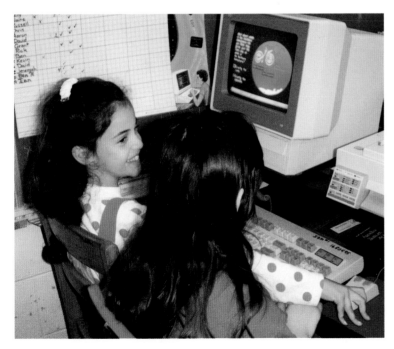

Students from Dommerich Elementary School in Maitland, Florida, use Prodigy to learn about wind and water currents.
[Susan Jennings]

Students can "Send Note to Boat" via Prodigy.
[Susan Jennings]

In Pursuit of Northern Light

```
Dear Rich and Bill,
I am a student following your voyage. I would like
to know about your background, your mental, phys-
ical and emotional strengths and weaknesses and how
you work as a team.

                            Good luck,
                            Paulo

Dear Paulo,
Few teams are faced with the constraints that we
have. There are only two of us working together on
an event which will take 1,830 hours. It's like
playing a decade of NBA seasons, games, and prac-
tices, all at once. Plus, we must live together in
a tiny cabin. If we become frustrated with each
other, as we both have, we must communicate that
carefully since there is no way to "get away from
it all." Each week, we talk about any aggravations,
record-attempt-related or personal, that we have,
so that these will not build up and become detri-
mental to our effort.
     Bill is usually even-tempered, but I run
more emotionally intense. That intensity is the
only reason we were able to actually get this
project together and be out here, so it was abso-
lutely necessary. And yet sometimes it makes things
harder here, when I become frustrated, like the
other day when we had let ourselves slip way to the
west of where I wanted to be on the path south. We
gave away about a day in that.
                            Cheers,
                            Rich
```

My coskipper on *Great American II* was Bill Biewenga, an experienced offshore sailor from Newport, Rhode Island, who was very excited about our school program. We would be taking turns sailing the boat and would share extremely cramped quarters, so it was important that we got along well. Since I was the skipper, all major changes and decisions would fall into my lap. But I knew that when Bill was on watch, he'd be sailing the boat his way. We were placing our lives in each other's hands.

GA II was 53 feet long and 45 feet wide. Picture a tennis court and then imagine trying to sail one. Our cabin was only 8 by 12 feet, so space was a major problem. We slept (or tried to) in bunks that were little more than large shelves. In heavy seas, to protect ourselves from bumps and bruises (or even concussions), we sometimes used pillows above as well as below our heads. The only place inside the cabin where we could actually stand was by the tiny sink.

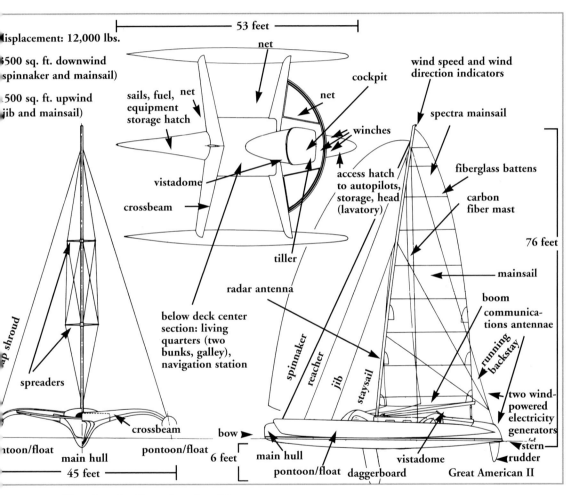

Displacement: 12,000 lbs.

3500 sq. ft. downwind
(spinnaker and mainsail)

1500 sq. ft. upwind
(jib and mainsail)

53 feet

net

sails, fuel, net
equipment
storage hatch

net

cockpit

winches

wind speed and wind
direction indicators

spectra mainsail

fiberglass battens

carbon
fiber mast

vistadome

crossbeam

access hatch
to autopilots,
storage, head
(lavatory)

tiller

radar antenna

below deck center
section: living
quarters (two
bunks, galley),
navigation station

76 feet

mainsail

boom
communica-
tions antennae

spinnaker

reacher

jib

staysail

running
backstay

two wind-
powered
electricity
generators

stern
rudder

shroud

spreaders

crossbeam

main hull

pontoon/float

45 feet

bow

6 feet

main hull

pontoon/float

daggerboard

vistadome

Great American II

The plans for Great American II.

[Nigel Irens, designer]

Bill and I in the cockpit.

[Stephen Rose/Boston Globe]

Great American II
BOSTON

Our need for personal space was less important than the need for storage. We had to carry not only supplies such as clothing (appropriate for extreme changes in climate) and food (we needed about twice the normal amount of calories each day), but also computer, navigation, and radio equipment, spare parts, and emergency equipment.

Everything had to be as compact as possible. We brought 200 Granny Smith apples, 200 oranges, and 12 dozen eggs. Since we had no refrigerator and other fresh food spoils quickly, we stored mostly dehydrated and canned food. We carried no fresh water, relying on a desalinator to make sea water drinkable. Also, we would be collecting fresh water whenever it rained to use for bathing and laundry.

```
Dear Rich and Bill,
I have 3 questions. First, how do you do your laundry?
What kind of clothes did you bring with you? And final-
ly, do you guys take showers or baths? If so, how?
                                    Cristianne, Age 13

Dear Cristianne,
When the weather is warm enough, we are able to go on
deck and shower by throwing a bucket of salt water over
our heads, lathering up, and rinsing with a few more
buckets of water from the ocean. For a final rinse, we
might use a quart of fresh water if there is enough to
spare. And when we took showers in the cold water of
52 degrees south latitude, we heated the fresh water
on the stove before using it.
        We do our laundry by hand, using water taken
from the ocean in a bucket. However, it's a rather
time-consuming process. So we don't do laundry as often
as we would on shore. Most of our clothing is made out
of synthetic fibers, which dry much faster than natu-
ral fibers like cotton or wool when washed in salt
water.

                                    Cheers,
                                    Rich
```

Facing page: *GA II*'s cabin contains a bunk on each side and the navigation station in the middle, with chart table, GPS (Global Positioning System—a system of satellites that broadcast signals which permit a very accurate position to be calculated), weatherfax, radar, telex, SSB (Single Side Band radio—a long-distance radio covering thousands of miles, for voice messages), VHF (Very High Frequency radio, used for communications over short distances of up to 50 miles), performance instruments, and electrical panel. The inside steering is on the upper right, in the "vistadome." [Billy Black]

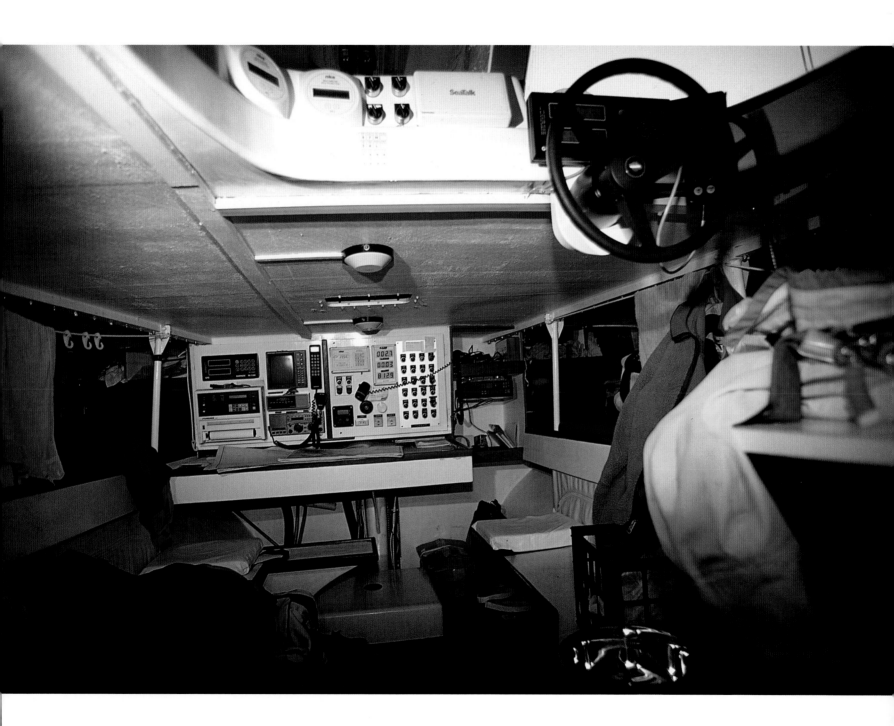

At last, the planning was completed and we were ready to go. After a wonderful send-off from family, friends, and the city of San Francisco, we sailed beneath the Golden Gate Bridge and headed south. A storm was forecast, but the wind increased more rapidly than we expected. It wasn't long before *GA II* was being bashed around by steep waves, as though riding a bucking bronco.

Early the next morning, only eighteen hours after we'd left, a vicious wave reared up, crashed into and over *GA II*. When the water drained off, and we could survey for damage, we saw that the front eight feet of her port pontoon were gone. We had no fear of sinking, but we could not continue toward Cape Horn without that bow. Stunned, we limped back to San Francisco.

Our eagle (emblazoned on the bow) leads us south in the late afternoon. [Bill Biewenga/Stock Newport]

Facing page: The broken bow acts as a huge scoop. When it dug in, it shocked *GA II* into a horrible shudder. [Bill Biewenga]

But there was never any question of giving up at that point. Thanks to an incredible team effort, a new bow was built, attached, and painted in only nine days.

We set out again and headed south for Boston. As we sailed, the Equator and Southern Hemisphere called us onward.

Facing page: Scaffolding and tarpaulins provide a sheltered workspace for the repair job.
[Patrick Short]

GA II passes under the Golden Gate Bridge under shortened sail. We had no time to paint our eagle on the new port bow.
[Patrick Short]

25

Dear Rich and Bill,
How do you handle waste like garbage and body wastes?
David

Dear David,
Anything biodegradable, i.e., paper products and cans,
is thrown overboard. Anything plastic (including those
little juice drink boxes, which have plastic between
the paper and the aluminum foil layers) is saved and
will be disposed of in Boston. Great American II has a
head (toilet) in the aft lazarette next to the rudderpost. Offshore, all body wastes are pumped overboard.
Cheers,
Rich

Eventually, we settled into a routine of five hours on watch and five hours off (Bill and I alternating time on deck). Sleep, or even relaxation, wasn't easy. People imagine sailing to be so peaceful, and often it is, but sometimes the noise can almost drive you crazy. Waves crashed, sails and cables slapped, water rushed by the boat, and the windchargers that generated our electricity spun so fast at times they began to howl, and we'd have to shut them down. You have to develop very sharp hearing out there, listening for whatever might be wrong.

Maintenance of good nutrition was as important to success as maintenance of the boat. [Bill Biewenga/Stock Newport]

Adjusting the main sheet, while the windchargers whir at the stern.
[Bill Biewenga/Stock Newport]

27

For example, I began to hear a sudden, unsettling *tap tap tap* from under the boat as we headed toward the Equator. *Oh no, what was that?* We didn't want to stop to look because we were trying to get out of the way of an approaching storm. Finally, after two days of hearing and worrying about that sound, I grabbed my diver's mask, tether, flashlight, and knife and jumped into the cold, blue Pacific. It was during a calm, and the water was at least 12,000 feet deep. I couldn't help but wonder what might be down there waiting to nibble on my toes.

Swimming under the boat, I got my first sight of the *thing* hanging from the daggerboard, long "arms" trailing. I had to wonder, *is it alive?* No wonder mariners of old believed in sea serpents. The culprit was actually two 18-foot pieces of kelp, 3 inches thick, caught and dragging on our daggerboard. It took me a long time to cut it all away.

That night, trimming the jib with my headlight on, suddenly *whump*, just beneath my chin, then *flap-flap-flap*. I had been hit by a flying fish! It was 6 inches long and 2 inches across, with a 6-inch "wingspan." Flying fish escape predators by leaping out of harm's way and gliding for up to 75 yards! This one was only the first of hundreds that were scared out of the water by the trimaran and mistakenly flew aboard. I tossed it back in, wondering which of us was more stunned.

Facing page: Back aboard after swimming under
GA II to pull giant kelp off the daggerboard.
[Bill Biewenga/Stock Newport]

Flying fish crashed aboard regularly. This one was
six inches long, with a six-inch "wingspan."
[Bill Biewenga/Stock Newport]

Conditions change quickly at sea, so we both had to be constantly alert. Whenever we hit heavy winds, we had to guard against *GA II*'s great bursts of speed by reducing sail. The danger when a trimaran goes too fast is that it can bury its bows, trip over them, and somersault. You never know what's going to happen next, and this causes incredible emotional strain.

At one point, off the coast of Chile, we were under siege in 40- and 50-knot winds for five days straight. The boat took a terrible beating, and we did too, rattling around in the cabin or cockpit. Even putting on clothes, eating, or brushing your teeth can be treacherous with all that motion; you find yourself suddenly tossed against a bunk or stabbing yourself with a fork or toothbrush.

It wasn't long before fatigue became a serious issue. We were getting only about three hours of sleep daily, and when you're that tired, it's easy to make mistakes. Even the smallest error can mean disaster. Since only one of us was running the boat at any given time, we each worried not only about our own performance but also, helplessly, about the other guy's.

This staysail rolls up like a windowshade. I marked it every foot along the bottom so that we could easily duplicate a previous setting.
[Rich Wilson]

Every morning we tied on a new American ensign and at day's end, we took it down and marked it with the day's latitude and longitude. We gave these to special friends afterward.
[Bill Biewenga/Stock Newport]

31

Cape Horn . . . Again

Dear Rich and Bill,
Are you getting scared as you approach Cape Horn where you encountered the big storm and crashed on your last trip? If you are, how do you handle this fear?

We wish you good luck on your voyage. We hope you reach your destination.

Sincerely,
Joni, Winslow, Eathan, Stacey, and Scott

Dear Joni, Winslow, Eathan, Stacey, and Scott,
I was very afraid before we capsized on Thanksgiving Day 1990! The waves were huge, immense, like a 6-story building. But at some point, you just have to say to yourself OK, there is fear here but it is not helping the situation. What will help?. . . Maybe it is keeping a lookout, or eating so you don't get weak, or putting on extra clothes so you don't get chilled and weak.

And when you do go out to do the scary job, you must absolutely concentrate on the task at hand, like getting the wrench onto the bolt and turning it one turn at a time, and not clutter your mind with things that won't help, like, I hope the huge wave doesn't break onto my head right now!

But the fear out here isn't really any different from other fears or anxieties on land. Whenever you extend yourself, or try something new, where the outcome is uncertain, there will likely be anxiety or nervousness.

I don't think many people are immune to that. Certainly, I am not.

Cheers,
Rich

The last time I'd approached Cape Horn, conditions couldn't have been worse. This time, King Neptune appeared to be smiling on us. We were able to move fast and stay ahead of a big storm and cold front. Within 900 miles of the Horn, I watched the brooding gray and black clouds with dread, but the seas stayed quiet. Two albatross wheeled overhead—a good omen, I thought. I fought my fear of facing the same spot where I'd almost lost my life.

On March 2, 1993, at 3:17 A.M., I saw Cape Horn's white, blinking light dead ahead. I was awed by the sight of a landmark I'd read about my whole life and by the mountainous coastline around it rising from the cold ocean, swirled in mist. Green and lush, yet windswept, the Horn is a place where nature is clearly in charge. I knew firsthand that it could get nasty without warning. So, putting our excitement aside, we wasted little time getting around to the other side of South America, into the lee of the continent. What a relief!

This albatross soared with us for several days. A student online on Prodigy answered our question about what albatross eat—squid!
[Bill Biewenga/Stock Newport]

GA II's repaired bow leads us past Cape Horn.
[Rich Wilson]

Yet I felt no certainty of success. Boston was still 8,000 miles away, after all. Major milestones such as the Equator in the Pacific, Cape Horn, and the Equator in the Atlantic are useful as symbols. They energize the spirit, but they don't win the race. Between these symbolic turning points are countless smaller ones, the hour-to-hour details of steering, trimming, reefing, cooking, stitching, lubricating, navigating, making repairs. Neglecting these could lead to a destroyed sail, an injury, a man overboard, an irreparable mechanical failure.

It was these small turning points in our journey that added up to make the big ones possible. And got us closer to Boston.

It was cold, cold, cold at the Horn, and after rounding it we headed due north for warmer latitudes. As if King Neptune knew we could use a little celebration, he gave us one.

Bill steering at Cape Horn.   [Rich Wilson]

Facing page: Sensing a sluggishness on the starboard side, I discovered that a small leak had let 500 pounds of water into the forward compartment. It was duly delivered back to the ocean where it belonged.
[Bill Biewenga/Stock Newport]

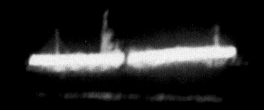

That night, when I was on watch, the horizon began to glow with bright, bluish-white lights and I came on a fleet of fishing boats (the lights attract squid). It was a wild scene in a black night. Needing a little fun, I put a spotlight on our sail, and then went tearing past one ship after another at about 14 knots. The men were running aft to see the bizarre spectacle. There I was, on deck in full foul weather gear and headlight, just two eyes peering out, waving at them and jumping up and down as we streaked past. The men waved back and watched the mystery sailboat disappear into the night again.

Throughout the voyage, we'd been in constant touch with our office in Boston and with students and others tracking us. Just past Cape Horn, however, we found that the connection to our radio antenna had broken. Repairing it required the two of us to hang off the stern of the boat, strapped into harnesses, in the middle of the night, while the boat charged along.

A fishing vessel off the Falkland Islands focuses huge banks of lights down into the water to attract squid. [Rich Wilson]

Tuning our long-range radio late at night. *GA II*'s cabin had no heater, and the cold in the deep southern latitudes was draining.
[Bill Biewenga/Stock Newport]

Not long after that, off the coast of Uruguay, our telex transmitter stopped. We had been transmitting our newspaper columns and Prodigy logs directly from our laptop computer through the telex, up to a satellite, and back to a land receiver. I tried to fix the telex for a week but couldn't. Then, our ham radio friends, with whom we had been occasionally talking, said that they would help. Every day until we reached Boston they were on the air to help relay our messages. What great friends!

Within ten days we went from the cold of the Cape to the intense heat off Brazil. The brilliant sun beat down on the boat. Dull and achy with fatigue, I actually fell asleep while steering the boat and collapsed face first into the cockpit. As if our discomfort wasn't motivation enough, there was the race itself. We knew that *Northern Light* had really turned on the speed in the Atlantic. We were ahead, but not by much.

Unfurling the huge spinnaker back in the tropics.
[Bill Biewenga/Stock Newport]

Boston on the Bow

Dear Rich and Bill,
I want to know if Northern Light meant to set a record or did it just happen?
                                    Good luck,
                                    Brad

Dear Brad,
Northern Light left San Francisco in company with two New York clippers, Contest and Trade Wind. These voyages were clearly a mixture of commerce and sport. The captains were proud and always wanted to beat other ships. Those voyages were touted in the San Francisco press as a race.
        It is said that Northern Light caught Contest off Cape Horn and passed her, with Captain Hatch shouting over to his rival that he "couldn't hold back his steed."
        Northern Light beat Contest by three days and Trade Wind by eight.
                                    Rich

Another encouraging turning point: after 11,000 miles of sailing, we finally turned the corner of Brazil and headed *toward* Boston. I radioed home: "We finally have Boston on our bow. Keep the porch lights on, Mom. We're coming home!"

Yet the challenges continued. Countless, unpredictable wind changes. The boat going 3 knots one minute, 23 knots the next. Storms and squalls requiring all sails down. Turbulence, through which all we could do was zigzag and lose time. Doldrums near the Equator, going in circles, no wind, putting sails up and down trying to get the boat moving, watch-

Just one half of a huge, complete end-to-end rainbow. A second full rainbow appeared on top of this one!
[Bill Biewenga/Stock Newport]

Facing page: Dolphins lead *GA II* toward the far horizon.
[Bill Biewenga/Stock Newport]

ing our lead over *Northern Light* dwindle. Then, whenever conditions allowed, risking too much speed in order to make up lost time.

These days were full and exhausting. But they were also, at times, magical. Like the day we saw a full, double rainbow, end-to-end. What an amazing sight! Or the thrill of 100 dolphins racing alongside us, tearing up the ocean and doing somersaults. Or the mystery of a hazy horizon and a thin, powdery dust covering our sails and ropes. Where could dust be coming from in the middle of the North Atlantic? I'd often heard about the Harmattan—a wind that sometimes blows dust from the Sahara Desert across the ocean. And that's what that dust was—sand from the Sahara, over 2,000 miles away!

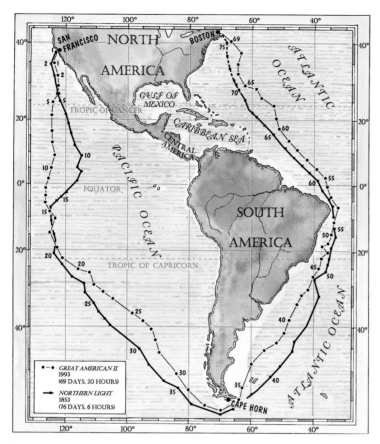

[Dennis O'Brien]

temperatures far warmer than those of the surrounding ocean water. The contrast in temperature wreaks havoc in the air above, and squalls and storms are commonplace. The Gulf Stream gave us a tumultuous ride through its spinning 100-mile-wide eddies and turbulent wave conditions.

Near George's Bank (off Cape Cod), the water is suddenly shallower and colder, and we got beat up badly by steep cresting seas of 12 to 15 feet. A lot of water came across the deck, and we felt some panic at the thought of not being able to keep the boat together during the final hours.

And it was so cold, a far cry from the heat of several days earlier. My hands felt as though someone were slicing them up with razor blades as I worked the ropes on the sails.

My hands were painfully beat up after nearly ten weeks at sea.
[Rich Wilson]

After sixty days out there, we were really wearing down, boat and crew alike. No matter how many miles still stretched ahead, I kept my spirits up by reminding myself that "Boston's on the bow."

We always knew that the last couple of days coming into the New England waters in late winter might be a real challenge, even after 15,000 miles and Cape Horn, and they certainly were. The Gulf Stream is like a river winding through the ocean, with water

Every night presented a unique sunset—some beautiful and inspiring, some dark and foreboding. [Bill Biewenga/Stock Newport]

43

Victory

April 7, 1993. What an unforgettable day! It was on this beautiful, clear day that *GA II* sailed off George's Bank and approached Boston Harbor. As we got closer to the finish line, we saw a ferry boat filled with about 200 people—family, friends, and journalists—coming out to greet us. The tugboat *Karen Tibbetts* formed a finish line with the Boston Lighted Buoy and fired a cannon as *GA II* crossed. We'd done it! We'd sailed ourselves and our boat safely to Boston and had broken the old clipper ship's record by six days! Our dream had come true! Everyone was in a mood to celebrate.

Entering the harbor, we found ourselves with an ever-expanding escort, including a Coast Guard vessel, a state police power boat, a harbormaster's boat, and a dozen spectator boats. As we came closer to where we were docking, I saw a crowd of about 1,000 people—many of them children—and wondered what was going on. I didn't realize, at first, that the crowd was there to welcome us home.

GA II **ghosts into Boston on a dying breeze.**   [Billy Black]

44

GA II crosses the finish line formed by the tugboat *Karen Tibbetts.*
[Daniel Forster/Stock Newport]

Boston's fireboat leads the way to the dock with a celebratory fountain of spray.
[Billy Black]

The wonderful team that had fixed our bow was there to take our docklines. Bill and I shook hands and gave each other a hug for a job well done. After affectionately patting the bow of *GA II*, we stepped onto land for the first time in ten weeks. It was good to be home.

For weeks afterward I was often stopped unexpectedly by people in the streets, calling out "Skipper" or "Rich" and wanting simply to tell me how much the voyage had meant to them or to their children. So many people all over the country felt they were a part of our journey, and to them it wasn't a distant adventure. It was as though they were all celebrating the fact that "our guys came home from the sea."

Less than a week later, Bill and I spoke to 550 students who had come to the New England Aquarium auditorium in Boston to meet us and to ask questions. This was the first of many occasions on which I was able to speak to groups of schoolchildren over the next several months, and I was always thrilled with the response.

That day in Boston, students raised their hands eagerly, and asked about goals, fear of failure, and limits. They asked for details about living on a boat for seventy days. And a teenager with chronic asthma told me she could never do what I did; later, however, she confided to a reporter, "If he did that, I can do anything."

I knew then that *both* our dreams had come true: offshore and onshore.

"Hi, Mom—this time we made it!" [Billy Black]

For ten weeks alone and far at sea, we had little idea that "our" adventure was becoming "their" adventure for many people on land.
[Billy Black]

Surrounded by a group of students whom we had tried so hard to reach and teach, we receive silver Revere bowls from the mayor of Boston.
[Billy Black]

Along Commonwealth Avenue in Boston there is a statue of maritime historian Samuel Eliot Morison, sitting on a rock and gazing out to sea. On the side of the rock is carved: "Dream dreams, then write them, aye, but live them first." To all who face challenges of their own, I say, *Keep dreaming your own dreams, and the day will come for you to go and live them.*

Glossary

Aft   Toward the back end of a boat.

Bow   The front of a boat.

Container ship   A ship whose cargo consists of 20-foot or 40-foot containers similar to those on tractor-trailers.

Daggerboard   A finlike board that slides up and down through a slot in the hull and extends down into the water. The daggerboard keeps the boat from slipping sideways as it sails. (See diagram on page 19.)

Doldrums   Very calm areas of the ocean where the wind is light and the sea is flat.

Eddies   Whirlpools formed by wanderings of the Gulf Stream.

Hatch   A small opening in the deck of a ship or boat.

Hull   The body of a boat, which rests in the water.

Jib   The triangular sail attached to the front stay that holds the mast up. (See diagram on page 19.)

Knot   One nautical mile per hour.

Lazarette   A storage compartment under the deck near the stern.

Lee   The sheltered, downwind side of a structure or land mass.

Nautical   Having to do with the sea.

Nautical chart   A printed map used by navigators, which represents a small or large area of water, providing many details such as the location of buoys, lighthouses, rocks, shoals, wrecks, underwater cable, etc.

Neoprene   A form of rubber that is resistant to abrasion and salt water.

Pontoon   The outside hull of a trimaran. (See diagram on page 19.)

Reefing   Reducing the area of a sail when the wind strength increases.

Rudderpost   A vertical and pivoting post that goes from the deck, through the lazarette, through the bottom of the boat, and into the water. The rudder is attached in the water and the steering systems are attached inside the boat. (See diagram on page 19.)

Squalls   Small, intense storms that may bring high winds for brief periods.

Stern   The back of a boat.

Trimaran   A boat with three hulls attached with crossbeams. The outside hulls keep the boat upright.

Trimming   Pulling in or letting out the sails so that they are always full of wind.

Index